# FEATHERED FRIENDS

## Stories and Anecdotes about Our Avian Companions

### Philipp Frühwirth

# CONTENTS

# INTRODUCTION TO BIRDS: WHAT ARE BIRDS AND WHY ARE THEY IMPORTANT?

Birds are fascinating creatures that have intrigued humankind for centuries. They are warm-blooded animals with feathers and wings that enable them to fly. Birds are important for various reasons and have been significant in human history, culture, and scientific studies.

Birds play an essential role in the ecosystem. They act as pollinators, seed dispersers, and pest control agents, which are crucial for maintaining a healthy environment. Some bird species, such as the hummingbird and the eagle, are indicators of the health and balance of an ecosystem.

Moreover, birds are significant sources of food and other resources. Humans have been hunting birds for their meat, feathers, and eggs for millennia. For instance, the turkey has become a popular meal during Thanksgiving Day in the United States. Besides that, birds are sources of inspiration for art and culture, making them an essential part of the human experience.

Birds also have unique abilities that fascinate people. One of these abilities is the ability to fly. Birds have wings that allow them to fly from one place to another, which is extraordinary when compared to other animals. The bird's wings are designed in a way that makes flying energy-efficient, allowing them to travel long distances with minimal effort.

Another unique ability of birds is their singing ability. Most birds are known for their beautiful and unique songs, which they use for various reasons. Some birds use birdsongs to attract mates, while others use them to mark their territory or communicate with their species.

Furthermore, birds have been the subject of scientific studies for decades. Scientists study birds to understand their biology, behavior, and ecology. Birds have been instrumental in shaping our understanding of evolution, migration, and other biological wonders.

In conclusion, birds are remarkable creatures that bring beauty and value to our lives. They are essential for maintaining a healthy ecosystem and contribute to our culture and history. Understanding and appreciating birds can help us become better stewards of the environment and promote the conservation of these incredible animals. In the next chapter, we will discuss the anatomy of birds in more detail.

# THE ANATOMY OF BIRDS: UNDERSTANDING THE DIFFERENT BODY PARTS

Birds have unique physical characteristics that enable them to fly and thrive in a variety of environments. Understanding the anatomy of birds is important for appreciating their diversity and for understanding how they function in the ecosystem. Here are some of the key parts of a bird's anatomy:

Feathers: Feathers are one of the most distinctive features of birds. They provide insulation, help birds to fly, and aid in communication and mating displays. Feathers are made of keratin, the same protein that makes up human hair and nails.

Beak: A bird's beak is its primary tool for feeding, grooming, and defense. The shape and size of the beak vary depending on the bird's diet and habitat. Some birds have curved, sharp beaks for catching prey, while others have strong, thick beaks for cracking nuts or seeds.

Wings: Birds have wings that are specially adapted for flight. They are lightweight and have a flexible, aerodynamic design that helps birds to generate lift and maneuver in the air. The muscles that power the wings are attached to a bird's breastbone, which provides a strong anchor for flight.

Legs and Feet: A bird's legs and feet are also adapted for its particular lifestyle. Some birds, like raptors and owls, have sharp talons for catching prey. Other birds, such as wading birds, have long, thin legs that allow them to navigate through water or marshy terrain. Each bird's feet have unique structures and adaptations that aid them in movement and balance.

Respiratory System: A bird's respiratory system is different from mammals in several ways. Birds have a system of air sacs that connect to their lungs, which allows them to breathe in a continuous loop rather than a back-and-forth flow. This adaptation helps them to extract more oxygen from the air and to sustain the high energy demands of flight.

Digestive System: Birds have a specialized digestive system that allows them to extract nutrients from a wide variety of foods. Many birds have a crop, a pouch-like structure in their esophagus that stores food before it enters the stomach. They also have a two-part stomach, the proventriculus which secretes digestive enzymes and the gizzard which grinds and mashes food for digestion.

Understanding the anatomy of birds is essential for appreciating their unique adaptations and roles in the ecosystem. By studying bird anatomy, scientists can better understand how birds fly, communicate, and navigate their environments.

# TYPES OF BIRDS: A GUIDE TO BIRD CLASSIFICATION

Birds come in different shapes, sizes, and colors, and there are a wide variety of species around the world. These species are grouped based on their characteristics and shared ancestry, making up what is known as bird classification, or taxonomy.

Birds are classified into taxa, which are groups or ranks in a hierarchical system of classification, starting from the largest to the smallest groups. The first major group of birds are the Ratites, a group that consists of ostriches, rheas, emus, cassowaries, and kiwis. These are characterized by their unique flat breastbones, which lack a keel, a structure that helps powers flight in other birds.

The second major group of birds are the Galloanserae, a group consisting of waterfowl, gamebirds, and several others. This group is distinguished by their fused bones in the pelvic region and lack of a crop, a sac-like structure at the base of the throat that is used to store food.

The third major group is the Neoaves, which contains almost all of the remaining bird species on earth. They are differentiated from other groups by their skulls and bill structures.

The Neoaves group contains several smaller groups such as Ciconiiformes, containing storks and herons; Falconiformes consisting of hawks, eagles, and vultures; and Passeriformes, the largest group of birds, which include perching birds such as sparrows, finches, and warblers.

There are also groups classified based on where birds are found, such as seabirds, waterbirds, landbirds, and birds of prey. Some birds are restricted to certain regions, such as penguins in the Southern Hemisphere or toucans in the tropical forests of South America.

Bird classification continues to be updated as new species are discovered, and advancements in genetics and DNA sequencing reveal new relationships between existing species. The classification system helps bird enthusiasts and scientists alike to identify, understand, and conserve these fascinating creatures.

# A BRIEF HISTORY OF BIRDS: EVOLUTION AND ORIGIN

Birds are some of the most fascinating animals that have ever existed. They come in various sizes, colors, and shapes, and have unique features that set them apart from all other animals. Over the years, scientists have sought to understand the evolution and origin of birds, and in this chapter, we will take a brief look at this fascinating history.

Birds are believed to have evolved from a group of theropod dinosaurs, which lived during the Jurassic period, about 150 million years ago. Theropod dinosaurs were bipedal carnivores that had evolved feathers, which they used for insulation, display, and to aid in movement.

The first bird-like dinosaur to exist was Archaeopteryx. It lived approximately 155-150 million years ago during the Late Jurassic period. The bird was similar to small theropod dinosaurs, but it had strong feathered wings that allowed it to fly. The feathers on the wings were symmetrical, and the tail had feathers, similar to the modern birds.

Over the years, birds evolved and diversified into more than 10,000 species, each occupying a unique ecological niche, from the tiny hummingbirds to the massive ostriches.

Birds are one of the few groups of animals that have evolved the ability to fly. The evolution of feathers and the development of the lightweight skeleton were significant adaptations that allowed birds to fly. The bird's wings are strong and capable of generating lift, while the tail feathers stabilize the bird as it flies.

Besides flying, birds have many other unique adaptations. For example, most birds have a keeled breastbone or sternum that serves as an anchor for the powerful muscles used in flying. Birds also have different beak shapes that correspond to their feeding habits. For instance, woodpecker's beaks are long and sharp to easily penetrate wood, while pelicans have long and wide beaks that they use to scoop up fish.

In conclusion, the history of birds is a fascinating subject that has captivated scientists and bird lovers alike for decades. The evolution and diversification of birds have resulted in the vast array of unique features, ecology, and behavior we see in birds today. Understanding this history can help us appreciate these amazing creatures and their vital role in the ecosystem.

# MIGRATORY BIRDS: WHY AND HOW DO THEY MIGRATE?

Migratory birds are a fascinating and diverse group of birds that undertake long-distance journeys to breed, feed, and survive. These birds face a number of challenges along their migratory route, including changing weather patterns, predators, and habitat loss. So, why do migratory birds undertake such arduous journeys, and how do they navigate this perilous journey?

The primary reason migratory birds undertake such migrations is to take advantage of seasonal changes in food, water, and weather. During the breeding season, many birds require specific habitats and food sources to successfully reproduce and raise their young. But these resources are not available year-round in one location. As seasons change, and food and water sources become scarce in one location, birds are forced to move to new habitats that offer important resources.

So, how do migratory birds navigate such long and complex routes? Scientists believe that birds navigate using a combination of internal compasses, visual cues, and magnetic sensing. Recent research has shown that birds are able to detect changes in the Earth's magnetic fields and use them to orient themselves during migration. Some species are also able to use the sun and stars to navigate, while others use visual landmarks such as mountains or coastlines to guide their journey.

While migration is a natural behavior for many bird species, it is not without its challenges. The loss of habitat along migratory routes, as well as climate change and other human activities, has made the journey even more difficult for many species. To help protect migratory birds and their habitats, conservation efforts have been put in place around the world. These efforts include the creation of protected migration routes, the restoration of lost habitat, and the regulation of hunting and other activities that can damage or destroy important bird habitats.

Despite the challenges, migratory birds continue to undertake their long journeys, providing a vital link in ecosystems around the world. Understanding why and how these birds migrate is an important step in their protection and conservation for future generations to enjoy.

# BIRD COMMUNICATION: SONGS, CALLS AND EXPRESSIONS

Bird communication is a complex system of sounds, gestures, and behaviors that allows birds to interact with each other and their environment. Birds use different vocalizations and physical movements to convey various messages, such as warning of danger, attracting mates, establishing territory, or coordinating with their flock. In this chapter, we'll explore the different types of bird communication, what they mean, and how they are used.

## Bird Songs

Bird songs are among the most recognizable sounds in nature. Male birds use songs to attract mates and defend their territory during nesting season, while some species sing all year round. Songs are usually loud, melodious, and repetitive, and some species have very complex songs, like the Nightingale or the Mockingbird. Each bird species has a unique repertoire of songs, and these songs can vary depending on the region or the individual bird.

## Bird Calls

Bird calls are shorter and simpler than songs, and serve different purposes. Calls are used by both males and females to communicate with each other and their offspring, and they can convey various messages, such as alarm, aggression, food location, or contact. Different calls often have different meanings, and some species have very specific calls for particular situations, like the Hawk's warning call or the Chickadee's contact call.

## Body Language

Birds also use physical movements and postures to communicate with each other. Some species have elaborate courtship displays, like the Peacock's fanned tail or the Bird of Paradise's dance. Other birds use body language to convey aggression or submission, like puffing up feathers or lowering the head. Some birds, like the Vulture, use their body language to regulate their body temperature by spreading their wings or exposing their legs.

## Conclusion

Bird communication is a fascinating and complex subject that requires careful observation and interpretation. By paying attention to the different sounds and behaviors of birds, we can gain insight into their social structure, ecology, and evolutionary history. Whether you're birdwatching or just enjoying the sounds of nature, take a moment to listen to the songs, calls, and expressions of the birds around you and discover the world of avian communication.

# BIRD BEHAVIOR: UNDERSTANDING THEIR HABITS AND PREFERENCES

Birds exhibit a wide range of behaviors, from breeding and nesting to feeding and flying. Understanding these behaviors can provide valuable insights into their habits and preferences. Here are some of the most common bird behaviors:

Breeding Behavior: Breeding season varies depending on the species and location. Some birds breed during the spring, while others breed during the winter. During breeding season, males often use elaborate displays to attract females, such as singing, dancing, and offering gifts of food.

Nesting Behavior: Nest construction also varies depending on the species. Some birds construct elaborate nests out of twigs and grass, while others simply lay their eggs in a depression on the ground. After the eggs hatch, both parents care for the young until they are ready to fledge.

Feeding Behavior: Birds have different feeding preferences and strategies. Some birds are carnivorous and hunt for prey, while others are herbivorous and feed on fruits and seeds. Some birds have specialized bills for feeding on nectar or insects.

Flying Behavior: Birds are well known for their ability to fly. Their wings are adapted for sustained flight, with feathers that provide lift and an aerodynamic shape that reduces drag. Some birds fly long distances during migration, while others remain in one area year-round.

Social Behavior: Birds are often social creatures and may

congregate in flocks during breeding season or for feeding or roosting. Some birds are monogamous, forming life-long pair bonds, while others mate with multiple partners.

Territorial Behavior: Many birds are territorial and defend their nesting or feeding areas against intruders. Some birds will display aggressive behaviors, such as vocalizing, posturing, or even attacking, to defend their territory.

Understanding bird behavior is essential for bird enthusiasts, ornithologists, and conservationists. By observing and documenting bird behavior, we can gain a deeper appreciation for the complexity and adaptability of these amazing creatures. It can also help us to better understand how birds interact with their environment and how we can protect them.

# BIRD WATCHING: TIPS AND TRICKS ON THE ART OF BIRDING

Bird Watching, also known as Birding, is a popular hobby enjoyed worldwide by millions of people of all ages. It is an excellent way to connect with nature, observe unique species of birds and their behavior, and enhance one's knowledge about birds.

Here are some tips and tricks on the art of birding:

1. Invest in a Good Pair of Binoculars: A pair of binoculars is an essential tool that can make a significant difference in your birding experience. It would help if you looked for binoculars that are durable, lightweight, and have excellent magnification.

2. Get Familiar with Your Camera: A camera is a wonderful birding tool that allows you to capture the beauty of birds in their natural habitat. Learn how to use your camera settings to get the best shots and try to practice shooting in different light conditions.

3. Learn to Identify Birds: One of the essential skills in birding is identifying different species of birds. You can learn the differences in their plumage, shape, and behavior to identify them. You can use field guides and online resources to help you identify them.

4. Find the Best Times to Go Birding: The best time to go birding is early in the morning when birds are most active. During this time, they are singing, foraging, and are generally easier to spot. The evening is another excellent time for birding since many birds are active at dusk.

5. Know Where to Look: To find birds, you need to know where to look. Parks, nature reserves, and forests are excellent places to

start. Look for habitats that provide food and shelter such as trees, bushes, and water sources.

6. Dress for the Occasion: Most birding takes place outdoors, and weather can be unpredictable. Dress appropriately for the weather and wear comfortable shoes. Avoid bright colors, as they can scare the birds away.

7. Respect Wildlife: When birding, make sure to respect the birds and their habitat. Do not approach nests or disturb the birds' environment. Stay on designated paths and trails to avoid damaging the surroundings.

In conclusion, bird watching is a great way to connect with nature and learn about different species of birds. The hobby requires patience and dedication but can be rewarding with the right attitude and preparation. Remember to enjoy the experience and appreciate the beauty of birds.

# THE ROLE OF BIRDS IN THE ECOSYSTEM: HOW THEY CONTRIBUTE TO NATURE

Birds play a crucial role in the ecosystem, contributing to the balance of nature in various ways. They are often referred to as environmental indicators and are good indicators of the health of the environment. Below are some of the ways in which birds contribute to nature.

1. Pollination: Some bird species such as hummingbirds, sunbirds, and honeyeaters are known to play a role in pollination. They feed on nectar and as they move from one flower to another, they transfer the pollen, thereby helping in the fertilization of plants.

2. Seed Dispersal: Some bird species such as hornbills, turacos, and toucans feed on fruits and berries, and as they fly, they disperse the seeds over large distances. This helps in the growth and distribution of various plant species.

3. Pest Control: Birds such as hawks, eagles, and owls are known to feed on rodents and other harmful animals, helping to control their population. This reduces the need for pesticides and other forms of pest control, which can have harmful effects on the environment.

4. Nutrient Cycling: Birds contribute to nutrient cycling in the ecosystem by feeding on insects, worms, and other small animals. They excrete waste products that are rich in nutrients, which are then used as fertilizer by plants.

5. Soil Aeration: Birds that feed on soil-dwelling insects and animals, such as thrushes and robins, help to aerate the soil

as they move around, which promotes healthy root growth and improves soil drainage.

6. Food Chain: Birds occupy various positions in the food chain and contribute to the overall balance of the ecosystem. They provide food for larger predators such as raptors and snakes and smaller predators such as cats and dogs.

7. Ecotourism: Bird watching and other activities that involve birds contribute to the economy of local communities through ecotourism. This not only provides an opportunity for people to appreciate the beauty and diversity of birds but also helps to raise awareness about the importance of conservation.

In conclusion, birds play a critical role in the ecosystem, and their presence or absence can have a significant impact on the environment. It is, therefore, essential to conserve bird populations and their habitats to maintain the balance of nature.

# THREATS TO BIRDS: HUMAN ACTIVITIES THAT ENDANGER BIRD POPULATION

Birds are an essential part of our ecosystem, playing an important role in pollination, seed dispersal, and insect control. However, human activities have led to a decline in bird populations and put several species at risk of extinction. In this chapter, we will discuss the threats to birds and how human activities impact their survival.

1. Habitat Loss and Fragmentation: One of the primary causes of declining bird populations is habitat loss due to urbanization, agriculture, and infrastructure development. As human populations expand, the natural habitats of birds are destroyed, and they are forced to migrate or adapt to new environments, which can lead to reduced breeding success and survival.

2. Climate Change: Climate change is a significant threat to birds, with rising temperatures affecting their habitats, food sources, and migratory patterns. Changes in temperature and precipitation make it difficult for some birds to breed at the appropriate time, and food sources can become scarce due to changes in plant and insect life cycles.

3. Pollution: Pollution is another major threat to birds, particularly those that rely on aquatic habitats. Oil spills, chemical contaminants, and plastic pollution can harm birds through ingestion or contact, leading to acute and chronic health effects.

4. Hunting and Poaching: Hunting and poaching of birds has been a long-standing issue in many parts of the world, with birds hunted for their meat, feathers, and other body parts. Hunting

and poaching can cause significant declines in bird populations, particularly for threatened and endangered species.

5. Invasive Species: Invasive species can displace native bird populations by outcompeting them for resources or by preying on them. Invasive predators, such as feral cats and rats, can significantly impact bird populations, particularly on islands where birds have evolved without natural predators.

6. Artificial Light: Artificial light at night can disorient migratory birds and interfere with their ability to navigate, leading them away from their intended routes and habitats. This can result in bird mortality and population declines for some species.

In conclusion, human activities pose significant threats to bird populations, leading to declines in many species worldwide. It is crucial to recognize these threats and take measures to reduce their impact, such as conservation efforts, habitat restoration, and sustainable practices in urban and agricultural areas.

# BIRD CONSERVATION: EFFORTS TO PROTECT AND CONSERVE BIRD SPECIES

Birds have played an integral role in our ecosystem for millions of years, providing valuable services such as pollination and insect control, seed dispersal, and nutrient cycling. However, human activities such as habitat destruction and climate change have caused a decline in bird populations worldwide. This has led to a global effort to conserve and protect bird species, both for their own sake and for the benefits they bring to the environment.

Bird conservation involves various efforts to protect and manage the habitats, populations, and diversity of bird species. One of the primary goals of bird conservation is to prevent birds from becoming extinct. The extinction of birds can disrupt entire ecosystems, leading to a decline in biodiversity and loss of important ecosystem services.

One of the most important efforts in bird conservation is the protection of habitats, including forests, wetlands, grasslands, and coastlines. These habitats provide food, shelter, and breeding grounds for birds, and protecting them can help maintain healthy bird populations. Governments, NGOs, and local communities work together to create protected areas and reserves where birds can thrive.

Another important effort in bird conservation is the management of invasive species. Invasive species can compete with birds for resources and wreak havoc on ecosystems. For example, the European starling, an invasive species introduced to North America, competes with native birds for nesting sites and food, and has contributed to the decline of some species of native birds.

Education and public awareness are also important in bird conservation efforts. By educating the public about the importance of birds and their life cycles, people are more likely to understand how their actions can affect bird populations. They can then take steps to change their behavior and reduce their impact on bird habitats and populations.

Bird conservation is critical for maintaining the health of our ecosystem and the services it provides. Protecting and conserving bird species not only helps ensure their survival but also benefits other species and the environment as a whole. By working to protect and conserve bird populations, we can help ensure a healthy planet for future generations.

# BIRD HABITATS: UNDERSTANDING THE DIFFERENT ENVIRONMENTS BIRDS LIVE IN

Birds can be found in a variety of habitats all around the world. Different species have evolved and adapted to suit different environments, allowing them to thrive in a wide range of conditions. In this chapter, we'll look at some of the different habitats where birds make their homes.

1. Forests: Birds that live in forests are often adapted for life in the trees. They may have strong, curved beaks for cracking open nuts or sharp claws for grasping branches. Many forest birds are also brightly colored, which helps them to attract mates or to signal their dominance over other birds in the area.

2. Wetlands: Wetlands, such as marshes, swamps and bogs, are important habitats for many species of birds. These areas are often rich in nutrients, providing plenty of food for birds such as herons, storks and ducks. Some birds that live in wetlands have long legs to help them wade through shallow water, while others have webbed feet for swimming.

3. Deserts: Desert habitats can be tough environments for birds, with limited water and food resources. Birds that live in deserts often have long, pointed beaks for digging up insects or seeds from the ground. They may also have specialized adaptations for regulating their body temperature and conserving water.

4. Mountains: Birds that live in mountainous regions must cope with harsh environmental conditions, such as extreme

temperatures and high altitudes. Adaptations may include stronger wings for flying in thinner air or specialized feet for perching on uneven surfaces.

5. Grasslands: Grasslands are characterized by large expanses of open, flat land, with relatively few trees or other types of vegetation. Birds that live in these habitats often have adapted for ground-dwelling, such as long legs for running or ground-nesting to better camouflage their eggs and young.

6. Oceans: Ocean habitats are home to a wide variety of birds, including seagulls, pelicans, and albatross. Birds living in these areas have special adaptations for diving, swimming, and catching fish like webbed feet for better swimming or strong beaks for catching fish.

Understanding the different habitats where birds live is an essential part of conserving and protecting these amazing creatures. It's essential that we work to protect these habitats so that birds can continue to thrive and play their important role in the ecosystem.

# FAMOUS BIRDS: ICONIC SPECIES AND THEIR ROLES IN SOCIETY

Birds have played a significant role in shaping human culture and society for centuries, and some species have become iconic symbols in various countries and cultures. From the majestic predatory eagles to the colorful tropical parrots, birds have fascinated humans since ancient times, inspiring art, literature, and music across cultures. In this chapter, we explore some of the most famous birds and their significance in human societies.

1. Bald Eagle: The national bird of the United States, the bald eagle, is widely regarded as a symbol of strength, freedom, and resilience. Known for its striking white head, curved yellow beak, and sharp talons, this predatory bird is often depicted on the country's currency, flags, and other official emblems.

2. Peacock: This large and colorful Asian bird is famous for its iridescent tail feathers, which it displays in a stunning fan-like pattern to attract potential mates. In many cultures, peacocks are associated with beauty, pride, and fertility, and they are often depicted in art and literature across the world.

3. African Grey Parrot: Regarded as one of the world's most intelligent bird species, the African grey parrot is famous for its ability to mimic speech and human sounds. These birds are regarded as popular pets due to their affectionate nature and remarkable communication skills.

4. Penguin: Adorable and unique, penguins are beloved by people worldwide, thanks to their distinctive black and white coloration and their quirky, waddling gait. Penguins are often featured in popular media, including movies, TV shows, and commercials,

and they are associated with traits such as playfulness, loyalty, and community.

5. Flamingo: Known for their vivid pink plumage and distinctive long legs, flamingos are an unmistakable bird species. These birds have been featured in fashion, art, and pop culture, and they are often associated with grace, elegance, and extravagance.

6. Hummingbird: With their tiny size, iridescent colors, and lightning-fast movements, hummingbirds are one of the most fascinating bird species. These birds are famous for their ability to hover in mid-air and fly backward, and they are often regarded as symbols of joy, energy, and perseverance.

7. Kiwi: This small, flightless bird is the national symbol of New Zealand and is famous for its distinctive long beak and soft, fuzzy plumage. Kiwis are regarded as shy and elusive creatures, and they are often associated with the unique biodiversity of New Zealand's natural environment.

Overall, famous bird species play an essential role in human societies, providing inspiration, companionship, and entertainment for people worldwide.

# THE ECONOMIC VALUE OF BIRDS: HOW BIRDS CONTRIBUTE TO THE ECONOMY

Birds are more than just beautiful creatures that grace our skies and entertain us with their songs. They also play a significant role in the world's economy. Here are some ways in which birds contribute to the economy:

1. Birding Tourism

Birdwatching is a popular activity all over the world, and millions of people travel to different parts of the world to observe various bird species. This has led to the growth of birding tourism, which contributes significantly to the economy. In the United States alone, birding generates an estimated $41 billion in economic output and creates over 666,000 jobs annually.

2. Pest Control

Birds such as hawks and falcons are great pest controllers. They help to control rodent populations, which can be a significant problem for farmers. By eating rodents, birds help to reduce crop damage and increase harvests, directly contributing to the economy.

3. Agriculture

Birds like the honeybee and other pollinators play an essential role in agriculture. They help to pollinate crops, which contributes to crop yields and indirectly contributes to the economy. Without them, crops like apples, almonds, and blueberries that require pollination would be severely affected.

## 4. Ornithology

Ornithology, the scientific study of birds, is another way in which birds contribute to the economy. Ornithologists carry out research on birds, which helps to develop new methods for bird conservation and management. Their work is essential in guiding policy decisions and developing management practices that ensure the continued survival of bird species.

## 5. Ecotourism

Birds and their habitats are popular attractions for tourists seeking eco-friendly destinations. This has led to the growth of ecotourism, which contributes significantly to the global economy. Besides observing bird species, tourists also participate in activities such as bird banding, bird ringing, and bird feeding.

## 6. Falconsry

Falconry, the sport of training birds of prey to hunt, is another way in which birds contribute to the economy. Falcons are trained to hunt game, which provides a source of entertainment for falconers who pay a fee to learn this ancient art.

In conclusion, birds contribute significantly to the economy from tourism to pest control, ornithology, agriculture, and more. It is essential to protect and conserve bird populations since their loss can have far-reaching economic consequences.

# BIRD NUTRITION: A GUIDE TO WHAT BIRDS EAT

Birds are some of the most diverse animals on the planet, and as such, they have a wide variety of diets. What a bird eats is determined by its species, its habitat, and its behavior. Knowing what birds eat can help you attract them to your yard or spot them in the wild. Here is a guide to what birds eat:

Seed-Eating Birds: Many small birds, such as finches, sparrows, and buntings, primarily eat seeds. They are commonly seen foraging on the ground or at bird feeders. These birds have thick, powerful bills that they use to crack open seeds. Sunflower seeds, nyjer seeds, and millet are popular seed choices.

Nectar-Feeding Birds: Hummingbirds and some other bird species have long, thin bills and tongues with specialized bristles that they use to sip nectar from flowers. These birds need high-energy foods like nectar and sugar water to fuel their metabolism.

Insect-Eating Birds: Birds that primarily eat insects are called insectivores. This group includes many songbirds, flycatchers, and woodpeckers. Many birds eat larvae, caterpillars, and other bugs, especially during the breeding season when they need extra protein for their growing young.

Fish-Eating Birds: Seabirds like gulls, pelicans, and terns have long, pointed bills adapted for catching fish in the water. Some specialized species, like eagles and ospreys, hunt freshwater and saltwater fish by soaring high above the water and diving to catch their prey.

Rodent-Eating Birds: Raptors like hawks, owls, and eagles have strong, sharp talons and beaks that they use to catch and kill small mammals. They commonly prey on rodents like mice, voles, and gophers.

Fruit-Eating Birds: Some birds, like thrushes and tanagers, have specialized bills that they use to eat fruit. These birds are important seed dispersers, as they help spread plant seeds in their droppings.

In general, birds require a mix of carbohydrates, proteins, and fats to thrive. A varied diet of seeds, insects, and small animals provides them with the nutrients they need to stay healthy. However, not all bird feed is created equal, and some foods can be harmful to birds. Avoid feeding birds bread, which provides no nutritional value and can cause digestive issues. Salted peanuts and sugary treats should also be avoided, as they can be harmful to some bird species. By providing healthy, natural foods, you can help ensure that the birds in your backyard stay healthy and strong.

# BIRD HEALTH: UNDERSTANDING COMMON BIRD DISEASES AND DISORDERS

Birds, just like humans and other animals, are also susceptible to various diseases and health issues. As bird owners, bird enthusiasts or bird conservationists, it is important to understand common bird diseases and disorders, their symptoms, treatment and preventive measures.

1. Aspergillosis: This is a fungus infection that affects the respiratory system of birds. Common symptoms include gasping, difficulty breathing or sudden death. Preventive measures include avoiding dusty environments, cleaning cages regularly and providing appropriate ventilation.

2. Psittacosis: Also known as parrot fever, psittacosis is a bacterial infection that can affect all species of birds, including humans. Symptoms in birds include respiratory problems, diarrhea and lethargy. In humans, psittacosis can cause flu-like symptoms, pneumonia and in severe cases, death. Proper hygiene and regular health checks for birds are important preventive measures.

3. Avian Pox: This is a viral disease that affects the skin and feathers of birds. It can cause scab-like lesions on the face, legs, feet and beaks. In severe cases, avian pox can cause blindness, respiratory distress and death. Vaccination and maintaining proper hygiene are important preventive measures.

4. Egg-Laying Problems: Issues with egg-laying can affect female birds, especially those that are not bred for laying eggs. Common

problems include egg-binding, calcium deficiency, and egg yolk peritonitis. Providing a balanced diet, enough water and proper nesting materials can prevent egg-laying problems.

5. Candidiasis: This is a fungal infection that affects the digestive and respiratory systems of birds. It can cause vomiting, diarrhea, breathing problems and reduced appetite. Candidiasis is preventable through proper hygiene, including cleaning of cage and feeding equipment regularly.

6. Beak and Feather Disease: This is a viral disease that affects the feathers and beaks of birds. It can cause abnormal feather growth, feather loss, and beak deformities. There is no cure for beak and feather disease, but preventing the spread of the virus through proper quarantine procedures and vaccination is important.

7. Gout: This is a metabolic disorder that affects the kidneys and joints of birds. Symptoms include swelling of the joints, frequent urination, and uric acid deposits. Proper diet and hydration are important preventive measures for gout.

In conclusion, understanding common bird diseases and disorders is crucial to the health and well-being of our feathered friends. It is important to have regular health checks by a veterinarian, follow proper hygiene practices, and provide a balanced diet and appropriate living conditions.

# BIRD BREEDING: HOW BIRDS REPRODUCE AND RAISE THEIR YOUNG

Birds are fascinating creatures that have many different strategies for reproducing and raising their young. Some species lay eggs and leave them to hatch and grow on their own, while others take a more active role in caring for their offspring. In this chapter, we will explore the different ways in which birds breed and the methods they use to raise their young.

## Bird Reproductive Anatomy

Before we discuss the details of bird breeding, it's essential to understand the reproductive anatomy of birds. Birds have a unique reproductive system that differs from mammals in several ways. Instead of a uterus, female birds have a single ovary and oviduct. The male bird's reproductive system consists of two testes, which are located near the kidneys.

The breeding process can start with courtship, where the male and female birds engage in various rituals such as displaying their plumage or singing songs to attract a mate. Once a mate has been found, copulation takes place, during which the male transfers his sperm to the female's oviduct.

## Types of Reproduction

Birds use a variety of reproductive strategies, depending on the species and their habitats. Some birds lay eggs in nests and leave them to hatch on their own, while others lay their eggs in water or soil. In some cases, both parents take an active role in incubating the eggs and caring for the chicks.

## Incubation

Many bird species instinctively incubate their eggs by sitting on them to keep them warm, protect them from predators, and ensure they receive the right amount of moisture. During the incubation period, birds may spend up to 90% of their time on the nest, only leaving briefly to feed or drink.

## Raising Young

Once the eggs hatch, the parents must provide food for their young until they can fend for themselves. This can involve regurgitating food or bringing prey back to the nest, depending on the bird species.

Some birds, such as eagles, hawks, and owls, are called altricial birds, which means that their chicks are born without feathers or unable to move around for the first few weeks of life. In contrast, precocial birds, such as ducks, chickens, and geese, are born with feathers and the ability to move around and forage for food shortly after hatching.

Conclusion

Bird breeding is a complex process that varies widely among species. Understanding the different ways in which birds reproduce and raise their young is essential for bird enthusiasts, conservationists, and researchers. Through careful study and observation of breeding behaviors, we can learn more about these fascinating animals and their contributions to the ecosystems in which they live.

# BIRD PHOTOGRAPHY: CAPTURING THE BEAUTY OF BIRDS

Bird photography is a great way to capture the beauty of birds and their natural environment. To capture stunning bird images requires skill, knowledge, and patience. Here are some tips and tricks to help you get started.

1. Choose the Right Equipment: To capture great bird photos, you need good equipment. Invest in a high-quality camera with a zoom lens. A telephoto lens is ideal as it helps you get closer to the birds without disturbing them.

2. Know Your Subject: Knowledge of the birds you are photographing is essential. Study their behavior, feeding patterns, and nesting habits. Knowing when and where to find them will help you capture stunning images.

3. Learn to See the Light: Light is a critical element in photography. Early morning and late afternoon are the best times to capture beautiful lighting. It creates interesting shadows and a warm glow that adds depth to your images.

4. Use a Tripod: A steady hand is important for capturing sharp images. Using a tripod will help you steady your camera and prevent camera shake. It is especially important for using longer lenses.

5. Get Creative with Composition: Experiment with different compositions to create interesting and unique images. Try using the rule of thirds or framing your subject with natural elements like trees, flowers, or rocks.

6. Practice Patience: Bird photography requires patience. Birds move quickly and can be difficult to capture. Wait quietly and observe their behavior. Let the birds get comfortable with your presence before beginning to photograph them.

7. Shoot from Different Angles: Experiment with different angles to capture unique photos. Try shooting from a low angle or from above. This will give you a different perspective of the bird and its environment.

8. Post-Processing: Editing your images can bring out the fine details, color, and contrasts of your photos. Post-processing can enhance your images, but be careful not to over edit. Remember, less is often more.

In conclusion, bird photography requires a lot of skill, patience, and practice. Knowing your subject and choosing the right equipment is important, but it is also about developing your creative eye and taking the time to get the perfect shot. With some practice and persistence, you will be able to capture stunning bird images that will amaze you and others.

# FAMOUS BIRD SANCTUARIES AND RESERVES: PLACES TO VISIT FOR BIRD WATCHING

**Introduction**

Bird sanctuaries and reserves are the go-to places for bird enthusiasts and wildlife lovers. These areas are typically designated protected areas where birds can safely reside and flourish. Additionally, they not only provide a habitat for the birds but also offer opportunities for visitors to observe and learn about different species of birds.

**Below are some of the most famous bird sanctuaries and reserves around the world.**

1. Keoladeo National Park, India

Keoladeo National Park is located in the state of Rajasthan in Northern India. The park is a UNESCO World Heritage Site and a must-visit destination for bird lovers. The park is home to over 230 species of birds, out of which over 50 are migratory birds that come from as far as Siberia.

2. Kruger National Park, South Africa

Kruger National Park is one of the largest game reserves in Africa, covering an area of about 20,000 square kilometers. The park is home to over 500 species of birds, including the African Fish Eagle, the Kori Bustard, and the Martial Eagle, to name a few.

3. Ebro Delta, Spain

The Ebro Delta is one of the most important wetlands in Western Europe, located in Northeastern Spain. The region is a popular bird watching spot, boasting over 300 species of birds, including hundreds of pink flamingos.

## 4. Doñana National Park, Spain

Doñana National Park is located in Andalusia, Southern Spain. The park is home to over 320 species of birds, including the Spanish Imperial Eagle, the Red-knobbed Coot, and the Marbled Teal.

## 5. Galapagos Islands, Ecuador

The Galapagos Islands are a volcanic archipelago located in the Pacific Ocean, approximately 1,000 kilometers off Ecuador's coast. The islands are a UNESCO World Heritage Site and home to several unique species of birds, including the Galapagos Penguin, the Flightless Cormorant, and the Blue-footed Booby.

## 6. Kakadu National Park, Australia

Kakadu National Park is located in Australia's Northern Territory and is home to over 280 species of birds. The park is home to several endangered species, including the Gouldian Finch.

## 7. Komodo National Park, Indonesia

Komodo National Park is located in Indonesia and is a UNESCO World Heritage Site. The park is home to a diverse range of wildlife, including over 150 species of birds, such as the Green Junglefowl and the Orange-footed Scrubfowl.

## 8. Okavango Delta, Botswana

The Okavango Delta is one of the world's largest inland delta systems, located in Botswana. The region is home to over 450 species of birds, including the African Fish Eagle, the Saddle-billed Stork, and the White-backed Vulture.

## 9. Torres del Paine National Park, Chile

Torres del Paine National Park is located in southern Chile and is home to over 100 species of birds. The park is a popular destination for bird watching, offering stunning views of the Andes Mountains and the Grey Glacier.

## 10. Borneo Rainforest, Malaysia

The Borneo rainforest is home to some of the world's most exotic and rare bird species. Visitors can spot species like the Bornean Bristlehead, the Hooded Pitta, and the White-crowned Hornbill.

## Conclusion

These are just a few of the many famous bird sanctuaries and reserves around the world. If you are a bird lover or wildlife enthusiast, be sure to add these destinations to your bucket list. Each of these locations offers a unique opportunity for birdwatching and helps you understand and appreciate birds' crucial role in nature.

# FUTURE OF BIRDS: WHAT THE FUTURE HOLDS FOR BIRD POPULATIONS AND CONSERVATION EFFORTS.

Bird populations are constantly changing and evolving, and as such, it is important to keep a close eye on their numbers to ensure their survival. The future of birds relies on the efforts of conservationists and individuals to ensure their habitats are protected and their populations are maintained.

Climate change is a significant threat to bird populations, as it alters their migration patterns and availability of food sources. As a result, conservationists have been working hard to protect and restore a range of bird habitats, including wetlands, forests, and grasslands. Effective habitat management can provide the necessary resources for birds to thrive, ensuring the continuation of their species.

Conservation efforts have also been focused on preventing the introduction of invasive species, which can outcompete and displace native bird populations. Invasive species such as the Indian Myna, European Starling or European Rabbit are often introduced intentionally or accidentally, and they can cause significant harm to ecosystems by preying on, outcompeting or displacing native bird species. Conservationists, along with government organizations and wildlife management groups, are working to control invasive species to minimize their impact on bird populations.

Bird education and awareness also plays an important role in conservation efforts. Educating people about the importance of birds in the ecosystem, the threats they face, and what can be done to protect them can lead to increased conservation efforts and enhance the public's appreciation and respect for birds.

Technology also plays a role in the future of bird populations. Advanced  technologies and tools like bird monitoring cameras, bird identification apps, and satellite tracking devices are enabling researchers to collect data on birds populations as well as understand their behaviour, migration patterns and the threats they face. Such technologies and tools are helping in developing more effective conservation strategies for ensuring the future of bird populations.

To conclude, the future of bird populations and conservation efforts depends on the dedication of the individuals who protect them. With a combination of research, education, and good management practices, it is possible to protect and preserve these beautiful creatures for generations to come.